NEUROMANIA

NEUROMANIA

On the Limits of Brain Science

PAOLO LEGRENZI

Professor of Cognitive Psychology,
University Ca' Foscari, Venice, Italy

CARLO UMILTÀ

Professor of Neuropsychology,
University of Padua, Padua, Italy

TRANSLATED BY
Frances Anderson

OXFORD
UNIVERSITY PRESS

OXFORD
UNIVERSITY PRESS

Great Clarendon Street, Oxford OX2 6DP

Oxford University Press is a department of the University of Oxford.
It furthers the University's objective of excellence in research, scholarship,
and education by publishing worldwide in

Oxford New York

Auckland Cape Town Dar es Salaam Hong Kong Karachi
Kuala Lumpur Madrid Melbourne Mexico City Nairobi
New Delhi Shanghai Taipei Toronto

With offices in

Argentina Austria Brazil Chile Czech Republic France Greece
Guatemala Hungary Italy Japan Poland Portugal Singapore
South Korea Switzerland Thailand Turkey Ukraine Vietnam

Oxford is a registered trade mark of Oxford University Press
in the UK and in certain other countries

Published in the United States
by Oxford University Press Inc., New York

© Oxford University Press, 2011

The translation of this work has been funded by SEPS
Segretariato Europeo per le Pubblicazioni Scientifiche

Via Val d'Aposa 7 - 40123 Bologna - Italy
seps@seps.it - www.seps.it

The moral rights of the author have been asserted
Database right Oxford University Press (maker)

First published by Oxford University Press 2011

British Library Cataloguing in Publication Data

Data available

Library of Congress Cataloging in Publication Data

Library of Congress Control Number: 2011922685

Typeset in Albertina MT by Glyph International, Bangalore, India
Printed in Great Britain
on acid-free paper by Clays Ltd, St Ives plc

ISBN 978–0–19–959134–3

1 3 5 7 9 10 8 6 4 2

PREFACE

This book tells a story—a story of our times but with its roots firmly embedded in the past, intertwined with the origins of psychology in the second half of the nineteenth century. At that time psychology started to take precedence over more traditional disciplines, principally philosophy. Concepts that philosophers and theologians had been debating for years, such as 'soul' and 'reason', were either absorbed (reason and rationality) or expunged from the field of scientific research and relegated to the status of personal beliefs (the soul). Now it appears that something very similar is happening in the area of the mind, traditionally the field of study of psychology.

At present, various disciplines described using the prefix 'neuro', which we will discuss further later, are attempting to supplant the concept of the mind. Basically, what is happening is that the knowledge accumulated over decades of psychological and neuropsychological study is being presented as a novelty under new names.

As we shall see in Chapter I, neuropsychology is perfectly capable of covering all aspects of the study of the mind–brain relationship. Why then is there currently a tendency to fragment it into other disciplines? Is it to give the impression that new branches of knowledge have come into being alongside psychology and neuropsychology? Often the appeal exerted by innovations, especially to the layman, can be attributed purely to their novelty. Today, new fields of research characterized by a short circuit between the traditional spheres of knowledge—such as economy, ethics, politics, and even theology—and the discoveries made regarding how the brain functions are appearing on the scene.

It might appear that the fragmentation of these traditional spheres of knowledge into new disciplines is simply the result of a fad generated by the way in which scientific research is currently divulgated—designed to attract and seduce those who are not experts in these fields. Our objective in this book is to show that it is a much more significant process, and that there is much more to it than meets the eye. Of course it could simply be the end product of rivalry between academic fields, between neuropsychology and psychology on the one hand and the new disciplines on the other. If that is the case, the issue will not go much further than the usual debate among specialists, but in our opinion the question is far weightier than this.

If, when reading the newspaper, the ingenuous layperson comes across an article that identifies the location in the brain that controls falling in love, he/she is inclined to interpret the state of falling in love as something which is 'biologically determined'. This is what articles in the popular press allude to when they 'show' the site of 'falling in love' or 'disgust', illustrated with colour photographs, located in a specific area of the brain.

We must not forget that today the definition of the relationships between mind and body, psyche and brain, can involve choices in the realms of social politics and well-being. If the body, or more precisely that part of the body which is the brain, becomes the system of reference, and new disciplines (on which we will expand in the following chapters) within that system of reference are propagated, cognitive processes must take a back seat and consequently social politics and well-being will also have to take a back seat. At this point, wittingly or unwittingly, we may tend towards choices influenced by the combination of various aspects due to the new technologies: aspects with a 'biological' basis (When does the brain start and stop functioning?), a 'cultural' basis (When do we decide that the brain has started and stopped functioning?), and even with 'political' overtones (Can I decide beforehand to have the life of my brain terminated if it ceases to function correctly?).

The subject of this book is also of general interest because the new neurodisciplines relegate to the background a point of view that was in vogue about 40 years ago, during the protests of 1968. At that time, the prevailing ideology held that world events were the outcome of a process of construction forged by many minds rather than just one, of actions dictated by social and cultural factors that moulded the daily round. Today things are very different because of the influence of the new disciplines created by attaching the prefix 'neuro' to noble and ancient spheres of knowledge.

Many elements intertwine in this story and together we shall try to disentangle and clarify them, tracing the history behind recent discoveries that are often presented without mentioning their origins and critical aspects. This is where we will start in the first chapter, examining the various concepts regarding the functioning of the brain, and tracking this enthralling adventure in the realms of research from its origins in the second half of the nineteenth century to the present day.

CONTENTS

I

At the origins of the mind–brain
relationship

Before neuroimages

In 1861 the French neurologist Paul Broca described a patient who, following a cerebral lesion, was only able to say 'tan'. The post-mortem revealed the presence of a lesion in a limited area of the left frontal lobe. Since then it has been a known fact that in right-handed humans language functions are located in the left hemisphere of the brain (in left-handed and ambi-dextrous people the representation of the language areas in the brain is a little more complicated) and that that region of the left frontal lobe (known since then as Broca's area) is responsible for the production of speech.[1] Broca's observation was considered to be the first clear demonstration of two principles on which neuroimages were to be based over 100 years later: the brain (the cerebral cortex, to be precise) can be subdivided into a large number of portions (areas) with different functions, which are independent of each other and can be isolated. In the case of the patient who could only say 'tan', the function that produces speech had been isolated, through absence, by the lesion.

The concept of areas of the brain performing specific and independent mental functions (areas with modular functions, to use an expression made popular by Jerry Alan Fodor in 1983[2]) was not new even in the nineteenth century. In fact, it had already occurred to Franz Joseph Gall at the turn of the nineteenth century (the notorious notion of phrenology).[3] His mistake was to have proposed rather improbable mental functions (at that time psychology was not sufficiently advanced to provide him with adequate information) and to have thought that the development of the areas of the brain could be deduced from the external configuration of the skull (the 'bumps'). He also thought that the more an area was developed, the more efficient would be the functions for which it was responsible. In other words, the bigger the bump, the better the function. For example, if the skull bulged at the area where 'prudence' (this was the type of mental function that phrenology dealt with) was considered to be located, then the person was sure to be very prudent. However, to do Gall justice, it must be admitted that the idea of the 'bumps' is less bizarre than might be thought. Modern palaeo-anthropologists attempt to infer the intellectual capacities of the predecessors of *Homo sapiens* by the marks left on the internal surfaces of the skull by the cerebral arteries, the courses of which provide information regarding the development of the areas of the brain they supplied. Therefore it could be said that we now study the concave side of the bump, whereas Gall studied the convex side—less of a difference than might be expected, given the bad reputation that still haunts poor Gall.

Throughout the second half of the nineteenth century, researchers studying the neural basis of mental functions (mostly neurologists, who today would be called neuropsychologists) examined patients with lesions of limited dimensions (localized or focal lesions, usually caused by vascular damage). The logic was the same as that applied by Broca. All mental functions depend on the activities of cerebral structures which are mostly independent of one another and quite precisely located. Brain lesions affect a limited number of functions—sometimes only one. By carefully analysing the patient's symptoms it is possible to discover the function normally performed by the damaged brain structure. If speech perception is selectively compromised by a lesion of the left temporal lobe, it can be deduced that the damaged area, when intact, is responsible for the transformation of acoustic stimuli into speech sounds. Generally speaking, examination of patients with focal brain lesions, if done correctly, can, at least in theory, reveal the neural basis of any mental function.

At the beginning of the twentieth century, the modular approach to the study of the brain was abandoned because the results obtained were unsatisfactory and contradictory, and it was substituted by a holistic approach.[4] The prevalent conception, which was also influenced by Gestalt psychology,[5] a new movement that did not consider the mind to be an agglomerate of specific functions, was of an equipotential brain (with the obvious exclusion of the areas responsible for the elementary sensorial and motor functions). The damage to the mental functions caused by cerebral lesions resulted from the quantity of brain matter destroyed (the law of mass action) and not from the site of the lesion (the specific function of the damaged module). The development of the thinking of Sigmund Freud provides an excellent example of the transition from the modular to the holistic concept.[6]

Freud attempted an academic career, first as a physiologist (studying, among other subjects, the reproductive system of the eel) and later as a neurologist. His contributions to neurology were mostly in the field of language disorders (the aphasias) and perception deficits (the agnosias, a term he himself coined). In his early days he adhered to the modular approach, and in 1895 he wrote a review entitled (in the English translation) *Project for a Scientific Psychology*, which was strongly influenced by this approach. Prudently, however, he decided not to publish it; it was eventually published after his death. In contrast, his book on aphasia was a crucial contribution to the rejection of the modular approach, which had been strongly criticized, in favour of the holistic approach. Subsequently, Freud had to abandon his aspirations to an academic career and concentrate on the problem of how to treat his patients (many of whom were ladies with hysteric symptoms who could not be cured with the electrical treatments that were in vogue at the time). To solve this problem, he invented psychoanalysis, but that is a story that has been told many times before.

Half a century later the situation changed again as the holistic approach had not produced the anticipated results. There was a return to the modular approach, which was resurrected and improved in the 1950s and early 1960s by the theoretical contributions of Hans Lukas Teuber (1955) and Norman Geschwind (1965).[7] Subsequently, the study of the neural basis of mental functions by analysing the disorders shown by patients with focal brain lesions (i.e. neuropsychology) reached full scientific maturity and led to the acquisition of extremely important knowledge. As all fields of human knowledge depend on the functioning of the brain, there is nothing to prevent the application of neuropsychology to disciplines such as economics, aesthetics, pedagogy, theology, etc. In fact, neuropsychology could have been (and was, to a certain degree) extended to these disciplines without the need to invent new terms by the pleonastic use of the 'neuro' prefix.

Later in this book we shall discuss in detail why the 'neuro' prefix is so appealing to non-experts. For the moment it is sufficent to note that the 1990s were designated the 'Decade of the Brain' by the United States Congress, with a significant increase in funding for research into brain mechanisms. Therefore it is not surprising that many found it hard to resist the temptation to add the 'neuro' prefix to disciplines that had never been concerned with brain mechanisms in order to take advantage of the funding on offer. However, it must be admitted that the attraction exerted by the brain cannot be ascribed exclusively to the desire to gain access to otherwise inaccessible funding. After all, the first decade of the twenty-first century was proclaimed the 'Decade of Behavior' without any new disciplines sprouting in this field.

The study of the neural bases of mental functions that play a role in, for example, economic phenomena (but also in many other disciplines) falls entirely in the field of neuropsychology, and while the contribution of the term 'neuroeconomy' is by no means clear, the risk of using it most certainly is. Mental functions are studied by psychologists, not by economists or neuroscientists. The term 'neuroeconomy' implies, more or less explicitly, the exclusion of psychologists. And if psychologists are excluded, who will indicate which mental functions are relevant to the study of economy? If neuroscientists and economists intend to take over the study of mental functions from psychologists, without possessing the appropriate specific competences, neuroeconomy will not progress far. Let us not forget that Gall tried to invent psychology and ended up producing phrenology. This observation is equally applicable to neuroaesthetics, neuropedagogy, neurotheology, etc. There has recently been a flurry of important studies in the field of the neural bases of the mental functions involved in mathematical cognition. Fortunately, no-one has yet thought to introduce the term 'neuromathematics'.

Although there was nothing to prevent the various 'neuro' disciplines from appearing years ago, it took the triumphant advent of neuroimaging techniques to act as catalyst for their introduction. It would have been impossible to foresee this development even as late as the mid-1970s when 'computerized axial tomography' (CAT) scanning, a structural imaging technique, was introduced.

An Italian pioneer

Few members of the general public who read about the remarkable discoveries made in neuroimaging studies know that although the equipment used is extremely advanced and in constant evolution, the logic on which it is based dates back to the nineteenth century. In 1956 the Italian writer and artist Carlo Levi, best known for his book *Christ Stopped at Eboli*, published another work with a title that perfectly sums up what we are about to describe—*The Future Has an Ancient Heart*. The 'future' he was writing about was communism and the 'ancient heart' was the term he used for the backward conditions of life in the Soviet Union. The story of the Italian physiologist Angelo Mosso brings the title of Levi's book to mind, even if the destiny of the 'future', communism on the one hand and the circulation of blood in the brain on the other, was to be very different.

At the end of the 1870s Mosso studied the variations in blood pressure in the cerebral arteries that accompany the contractions of the heart (the heart beat). In babies, these variations can be seen as gentle pulsations of the fontanelle, the temporary opening between the bones of the skull.[8] Mosso observed similar pulsations in two of his adult patients through openings produced by traumatic lesions in the frontal cranial bones. This is much less alarming than it sounds; just as in babies, the meninges and the underlying brain are protected by the scalp.

Mosso noticed that the cerebral pulsations in one of his patients, Bertino, became stronger when the man, a farmer by trade, heard the bells striking at midday. Another interesting observation was that the increase in the strength of the pulsations was not linked to variations in the pulse rate and blood pressure measured on the patient's arm. Mosso decided (though why he did so is not recorded) that the sound of the bells reminded Bertino that it was time to say a prayer. Bertino confirmed that this was in fact the case. Therefore it followed that remembering that it was time to say a prayer caused a variation in the blood flow to a region of the brain. With this observation Mosso launched the process that was to lead to modern neuroimaging (possibly he was aware of having done so, although certainly he would not have been able to foresee how the process would develop) and founded neurotheology (and this he certainly would never have imagined even in his wildest dreams). To confirm the relations between mental functions and regional cerebral blood flow (rCBF), Mosso asked Bertino to do some simple multiplications in his head. The cerebral pulsations increased on both receiving the numbers to multiply and giving the answer. Who knows, perhaps Mosso discovered neuroarithmetic too!

From blood flow to mental functions

Newspapers and magazines often carry articles reporting that one research institute or another has found the area of the brain which governs falling in love or resisting temptation, illustrated by a picture of the human brain with a coloured section. The article explains that the coloured section is that part of the brain which becomes active when participants in the experiment see the face of their loved one or look at a cigarette they know they shouldn't smoke.

The reader is led to believe that, by using complex and sophisticated equipment, neuroimages will give a direct view of which parts of the brain are active while the person thinks about a particular object or desire. Most readers probably realize that the colour is simply a graphic device and the brain is not really coloured, but we cannot be completely sure of this. What we can be sure of is that the readers do not know that many steps are needed to produce that simple picture of the brain with a coloured area, and that each of those steps is based on assumptions which are not always sound.[9]

Using cerebral blood flow to obtain information about mental functions may seem rather a risky business, and in fact it is. Just one of the many problems that remain to be solved is the question of variations in blood flow which have a latency of 5 seconds or more (i.e. they take at least 5 seconds to get started). Human thought, even if not instantaneous as Descartes would have had it, has a latency of just a few tens of milliseconds. So how is it possible that very fast variations in thought are signalled by much slower variations in the cerebral blood flow? There is still no satisfactory answer to this question.

The steps that lead from blood flow to the mind can be described schematically. All mental functions and representations are accompanied by (or, more precisely, produced by) the activation of specific cerebral areas (remember the modular concept discussed above). When a specific mental function is operating, the cerebral areas involved are active. For example, if you are looking for a friend in a crowded room, the cerebral areas involved in orienting attention in space (located in the parietal lobe) and in recognizing known faces (located in the temporal lobe) will be called into play. If, like Bertino, you are trying to do multiplications in your head, the areas which govern the recovery of arithmetical facts (multiplication tables) will be activated. This is the long-term memory—that part of our memory in which we store knowledge permanently. The areas that process quantities will also be activated; these are also located in the temporal and parietal lobes, but they are not the same areas as those mentioned above.

Therefore we see that specific areas of the brain are delegated to specific functions (the visual search for a known face, or the multiplication of two numbers). Of course, many other 'generic' areas, which are responsible for operations that are common to many tasks (visual areas, acoustic areas, motor areas, …), are also activated. This is because visual and acoustic processing of incoming information and the execution of responses through the phonation muscles or the arm muscles are common to many tasks. The simultaneous activation of specific areas and generic areas presents a problem for neuroimaging research. However, scientific divulgation tends to highlight an area and give the impression that it is the only area delegated for a specific function, or even that it is the cause of a specific psychological effect.

The objective of all neuroimaging research is to identify the areas which selectively become active during any given task that requires the intervention of known mental functions. The cerebral areas are composed of a multitude of nerve cells or neurons (which we will examine later in this chapter), whose need for oxygen and glucose depends on the level of activation. The more active the cell, the more oxygen and glucose it needs. Oxygen (glucose is not as important in this context) is carried in the blood, which contains a high percentage of water. Therefore it follows that if the quantity of blood feeding the various areas of the brain at any given point in time is measured, it is possible to gauge the level of activation of those areas at that time. This is done by injecting a radioactive isotope into the bloodstream of a volunteer and then measuring the level of the isotope in the various areas of the brain using sensors placed around his/her head. The higher the level of the isotope, the more copious is the blood flow, indicating a greater consumption of oxygen which in turn signals a higher level of activation of the neurons in that cerebral area. Positron emission tomography (PET), which is frequently used today, is even more complex; the radioactive isotope emits positrons which collide with electrons, producing gamma rays which are recorded by sensors placed around the head of the subject. This is based on the same logic as the technique used by Mosso, although his method was much more rudimentary, i.e. measuring the flow of blood to the various areas of the brain through the strength of cerebral pulsations.

It is not considered ethical to inject isotopes into the bloodstream for research purposes, and so functional magnetic resonance imaging (fMRI), which exploits the water present in blood, is used instead. The volunteer's head is placed in a magnetic field (produced by magnets; hence the loud noise, well known to those who have had a magnetic resonance (MR) scan), which aligns the hydrogen atoms present in the water molecules circulating in the blood. When the hydrogen atoms come into contact with radiowaves they resonate, i.e. they emit a quantity of radiowaves in proportion to their number. The presence of a large number of hydrogen atoms indicates a high incidence of water, which in turn signals that the neurons are using large quantities of oxygen, indicating a high level of neuron activity.

At this point a word of explanation may be useful, although it is not related to what has gone before. Many of us have had a CAT or MR scan, but these are performed with different techniques to those used in research. They supply structural images of the organ under examination (not necessarily the brain); more precisely, they provide information on the anatomy and macroscopic lesions (if present), but they do not offer information regarding functions. On the other hand, the images produced by PET and fMRI provide information regarding function only or both structure and function, which has given rise to a new discipline, 'cognitive neuroscience', which covers both the studies that use neuroimages and those that are based on the analysis of the deficits of patients with focal brain lesions (classic neuropsychology).

Back to the 1800s again!

If we ask someone to do a multiplication in his/her head, as in the example in the previous section, and record the cerebral activity, the result is rather disappointing—almost all the cerebral areas are active. This shouldn't come as a surprise as what we are looking at are activations of different types: activation of cerebral areas on which the mental functions involved in the specific and non-specific aspects of the experimental task depend, and activation of cerebral areas that have nothing at all to do with the experimental task (after all, the volunteer will not be thinking exclusively about the experimental task). As the researcher is usually interested in identifying the regions of the brain that are selectively involved in the mental functions related to the specific aspects of the experimental task (e.g. the cerebral areas we use when doing a multiplication in our head), the problem is how to disentangle the activations in order to eliminate those which are not caused by the mental functions specific to the task in hand.

Various methods have been proposed to achieve this, and undoubtedly others will be proposed in the future (this research area is developing rapidly as it is of crucial importance for the interpretation of neuroimages). However, as stated earlier, the heart of the future is rooted in the past, and the most popular method to date is 'cognitive subtraction' which was proposed in 1868 by Franciscus Cornelius Donders, a Dutch ophthalmologist, to study mental functions with reaction times (the term used today is 'mental chronometry').[10] It is interesting to note that mental chronometry experienced the same fate as the modular approach discussed earlier; it was abandoned at the beginning of the twentieth century and then recovered and improved by Saul Sternberg in 1969.[11] There is a certain irony in the fact that neuroimaging studies, which are universally (and correctly) considered to be an innovative approach and which have revolutionized research on the neural basis of mental functions (stimulating enormous interest among laymen), are based on studies performed as early as 1868 (cognitive subtraction) and 1876 (measurement of regional cerebral blood flow).

Cognitive subtraction

The logic behind cognitive subtraction is very simple, but rather difficult to explain. The first, and crucial, step is to identify a control task which involves all the mental functions of the experimental task with the exception of those whose neural bases we want to identify. The person participating in the experiment is asked to execute the experimental task and the control task in succession. While each task is being executed, the activation of tiny regions (voxels) of the brain is measured. These regions are shaped like tiny cubes with edges of approximately 3 mm, and each contains a vast number of neurons. In this way an activation vector is obtained for both tasks, which in this case is a number vector which indicates the activation level of the various voxels. Then the level of activation obtained in the control task is subtracted, voxel by voxel, from that obtained in the experimental task. If the result is zero, the neurons in the voxel are equally active in both tasks. If the result is greater than zero, the neurons in that particular voxel are more active in the experimental task than in the control task. If the result is negative, the neurons of the voxel in question are more active in the control experiment; however, for technical reasons, the negative results of cognitive subtraction are not usually taken into consideration. Needless to say, an incorrect (or inappropriate) choice of control task (which is not infrequent given the complexities involved) results in erroneous subtraction and inaccurate conclusions as to the distribution of cerebral activation. Therefore, if the wrong control task is used in cognitive subtraction, the results of the research will be worthless and even misleading. Thus, when reporting the results of a neuroimaging study it is essential to indicate whether cognitive subtraction has been used and, if so, the nature of the control task.

Let us assume that we are interested in identifying which areas of the brain are selectively activated when carrying out a multiplication in the head. The experimental task could consist of the experimenter pronouncing two numbers aloud and asking the participant to give the result verbally. In this case the control task could consist of the participant repeating the two numbers out loud. Cognitive subtraction will only give a non-zero result for those voxels which correspond to the cerebral areas that become active during the multiplication task, i.e. the areas in which the mental functions that are selectively involved in multiplying two numbers are located.

However, it is not as simple as it sounds. The activation level of a voxel can also be influenced by chance factors that cannot be controlled by the researcher and which also influence the result of the cognitive subtraction, and so the result also depends on pure chance. Therefore the chance probability associated with the result of the subtraction has to be calculated for each voxel.

Let us return to those attractive pictures of the human brain, with coloured areas indicating the locations of the functions of falling in love and resistance to smoking (the reader has probably forgotten about them in the labyrinth of the sequence of operations that produce the coloured areas). A simple graphic device is used here. After all, a diagram of the brain covered with numbers is not the most effective way to get the message across to the public; attributing colours to the various levels of chance probability is much more efficient. The idea of being able to see the brain at work, which so greatly appeals to the layperson, is misleading. What in fact is represented is simply the result of a graphic device which transforms chance probability into colour and is then superimposed on a drawing of the brain. It should be kept in mind that the use of colour to indicate different levels of probability is also applied to methods other than cognitive subtraction. Later we shall see the consequences that this seemingly innocuous device has on non-experts.

The use of attractive colours in neuroimaging has probably played a crucial role in their appeal to the public. As Martha J. Farah wrote, 'A picture is worth a thousand dollars'.[12] After all, we must not forget that our brain is predominantly visual and, as in the other primates, contains a large number of areas with neurons that respond to visual stimuli. We are very susceptible to the impact of visual evidence. Who knows—if Broca and his followers had used colour to differentiate the cerebral 'centres' in which the cognitive processes were 'located' instead of the realistic and austere drawings that in fact they did use, there might have been an explosion of 'neuromania' as early as the end of the nineteenth century.

As we shall see later, an interesting study demonstrates the (dangerous) attraction of neuroscientific explanations on non-experts. It might be argued that even experts—neuroscientists themselves—are not immune to the siren voice of this attraction. Perhaps they too are fascinated by the coloured drawings, but they show their fascination in a more subtle way.

Recently, the use of statistical inference in neuroimaging studies has been debated. The researcher can never be completely certain about any of his/her results. In fact, any result can be attributed to chance, to the chance effect of independent variables that the researcher is unable to control. Therefore statistical inference procedures are applied at the conclusion of every research project in order to assess the degree of probability that the results are due to chance. A universally accepted convention stipulates that if the probability that a result has been obtained by chance is 5 per cent or less, that result can be taken to be real. However, if the probability that the result was obtained by chance is greater than 5 per cent, the result must be considered as being due to chance.

It is obvious that statistical inference is of paramount importance for having a paper accepted for publication in a scientific journal. Scientific contributions with statistical inference procedures that are not considered to be sufficiently sound are rejected. However, in two recent papers[13,14] it has been maintained that highly prestigious scientific journals, which normally reject out of hand papers with even slightly dubious statistical inference, have published articles concerning neuroimaging studies with more than dubious statistical inference. In other words, even expert reviewers assessing scientific papers for publication can be 'blinded' by fascinating neuroimages and fail to apply sufficiently stringent criteria.

Mirror neurons

Mirror neurons, discovered in the early 1990s by the Italian neurophysiologist Giacomo Rizzolatti, compete with neuroimaging studies for popularity among experts and non-experts alike. The research which collects data on the activation of individual neurons requires a brief introduction as it is very different from the types of research described so far.

At the same time as Mosso was attempting to measure cerebral pulsations, another Italian, the histologist Camillo Golgi,[15] introduced a method of colouring neurons for which he won a Nobel Prize in 1906. This work was of fundamental importance for studying neuronal structure under the microscope. Golgi maintained that the elements constituting the brain formed a network (the syncytium theory). He must have been rather annoyed by the fact that his method played a crucial role in demonstrating the validity of a rival theory of neurons, advocated by the Spanish histologist Santiago Ramon y Cajal. Never the best of friends, they had to share the Nobel Prize and during the award ceremony they bickered, principally because of Golgi's attitude. Today, if two Nobel Prize winners were to squabble during the award ceremony, undoubtedly we would denounce the perversity of the times (and maybe lay the blame on television).

In any case, Ramon y Cajal was right—the brain is composed of an enormous number of neurons, organized in long chains. Neurons are cells that transmit electrical impulses (to exchange information). The nervous impulses from neurons upstream in the chain are transmitted through the dendrites (relatively short appendages of the cell body, the soma) to the axon, a much longer appendage, and from there to neurons further downstream in the chain. The crucial event that gives rise to the nervous impulse is a change (depolarization) in the permeability of the membrane which surrounds the neuron. Depolarization allows the passage of ions from the exterior to the interior of the cell. The direction of ion flow is perpendicular to the direction of the impulse. Just as a flame runs along the fuse, in the case of the nervous impulse the depolarization of the membrane (which then immediately repolarizes) runs along the axon. Once the impulse reaches the end of the axon, it releases chemical substances which boost it, across the synapses, to the dendrites and the soma of the next neuron in the chain. The membrane of the dendrite is depolarized and the impulse continues its course from one neuron to another.

Since the differences in voltage produced by depolarization (and repolarization) remain constant, only the frequency of the impulses varies (i.e. the number of impulses per unit of time). The information transmitted by the neurons is coded in the frequency of their impulses (the discharge frequency). A characteristic of neurons is that they respond, i.e. they vary the discharge frequency (increasing or decreasing it) depending on what is happening inside or outside the organism. When we speak of active cerebral areas we mean that the neurons in these areas modify their discharge frequency. Microelectrodes (extremely small electrodes with a tiny tip that can be inserted into the brain and placed in contact with the neuron membrane) are used to measure neuron discharge frequency (they are applied to animals who are awake and free to move). In this way it is possible to investigate the responses of the neurons in experimental situations set up by the researcher.

In 1981 the Nobel Prize for Medicine or Physiology was awarded to Roger Wolcott Sperry, David Hunter Hubel, and Torsten Nils Wiesel. Sperry had investigated the functioning of the two human cerebral hemispheres after surgical separation, and Hubel and Wiesel had made a fundamental contribution to understanding how neurons work, particularly visual neurons. Each visual neuron is receptive to a particular characteristic of the visual field. This can be something very simple, such as a luminous bar at a given angle which moves in a particular direction or has a particular colour. Other neurons are receptive to much more complex stimuli such as a hand or a face. The general principle is that each neuron codes for a characteristic of the visual world to which it responds preferentially. If a visual neuron is active, it responds; this indicates that the stimulus to which the neuron is sensitive is present within the visual field. Mirror neurons code for very complex characteristics.

Rizzolatti,[16] in studies of the macaque monkey, discovered the presence of neurons in certain areas of the parietal and frontal lobes (primarily dedicated to programming motor actions) which become selectively active when presented with gestures having a particular goal. For example, a neuron becomes active when the monkey reaches out to grasp food with its paw and carry it to its mouth. It does not become active when the monkey does something else or (and this is of the utmost importance) grasps something which is not edible. What is extremely interesting, and explains why these neurons are called mirror neurons, is that this same neuron becomes active when the monkey sees another monkey or a human grasping food and carrying it to its mouth. The neuron becomes active even if the observed gesture is different—if the food is grasped and carried to the mouth by means of a utensil (e.g. tongs). It is obvious that it is the goal of the movement, whether performed or perceived to be performed, that causes the neuron to become active, and not the movement itself.

It has been demonstrated that it is not necessary for the entire trajectory of the movement to be visible; if the final part of the movement is screened from the monkey's view, the neuron still becomes active if the goal is clear. Acoustic mirror neurons are present in the same area that contains the visual neurons. These are activated by a characteristic sound associated with a gesture, which is rendered invisible by a screen. An example of this is the sound of nuts being cracked.

For ethical reasons it is not possible to record the activity of individual neurons in humans, but neuroimaging studies suggest that mirror neurons are also present in the human brain. These neurons explain how it is possible to understand the gestures of others: an observed goal-oriented gesture activates the same neurons that become active in our brain when we perform the same goal-oriented gesture. If the mirror neurons are unable to function correctly for some reason, we will have difficulty in understanding the aims of the behaviour of others. Therefore it is not surprising that it has been suggested that malfunctioning of the mirror neurons is fundamental to pathologies characterized by difficulty in forming relationships with others, such as autism.[17]

Before mirror neurons

The idea that our brain can resonate with external events and that this allows us to understand them predates the concept of mirror neurons. However, before mirror neurons were identified, it had no empirical support and nothing was known of the underlying cerebral mechanisms.

It is not easy to explain how humans manage to discriminate speech sounds. The most obvious explanation is that each speech sound corresponds to an acoustic stimulus and that there is a mechanism that translates each acoustic stimulus into the corresponding speech sound. By means of this mechanism, each time an acoustic stimulus has certain physical characteristics a certain speech sound is perceived, for example /a/. This may be true for vowels, but it is certainly not so for stop consonants (of which there are six in both Italian and English: /b/, /d/, /g/, /p/, /t/ and /k/) which have widely differing physical characteristics depending on the speech context in which they are found. For example, the /b/ in the Italian words *barca* (boat) and *carbone* (coal) has different physical characteristics. Therefore it is necessary to identify a mechanism whereby the invariance of /b/ can be perceived when it appears to lack a physical counterpart.

At the beginning of the 1960s Alvin Meyer Liberman proposed the 'motor theory of speech perception'.[18] According to this theory, we are able to perceive the invariance of speech sounds because our acoustic system transforms them into the motor program (of the phonation muscles) required to produce them. We perceive /b/ independently of the speech context in which it is located, because its physical characteristics trigger the motor program that produces the speech sound /b/. Therefore the invariance is not found in the physical characteristics of the speech sound, but in the motor program that produces it.

The similarities between the mirror neurons and the mechanisms implicit in the 'motor theory of speech perception' appear clear. In both cases, an external stimulus triggers an internal motor mechanism that can reproduce it. The conclusion to be drawn from this is that motor aspects of cognition are far more important for human thought than has been believed. It is also evident that it is extremely difficult to find something truly new in neuroscience despite the fact that it is a rapidly developing field of study.

How then has it been possible to give the impression that not just a new method, or a new field of research, but an entire anthology of new disciplines has come to light? In the next chapter we shall attempt to explain why these new disciplines, which have come into being on the strength of the 'neuro' prefix, have invaded the realms of knowledge.

II

Mind, body, and explanations
of behaviour

Increasingly often, the press offers explanations of human behaviour supported by drawings, photographs, and graphic descriptions of sections of the brain which show that part of our grey matter that is activated when we think about something or plan an action. We are told that how we behave depends on the functioning of certain neurons. We hear about new disciplines such as neuroeconomics, neuroaesthetics, neuroethics, neuropolitics, neuromarketing, and even neurotheology (over 20 000 results on Google—look at the second on the list!).

In our opinion this is not a transitory fashion. On the contrary, it may well be just the tip of an iceberg, of which it would be wise to judge the dimensions to avoid a collision and, more specifically, to avoid it opening a huge hole in our boat. The heart of the iceberg was formed long ago, in the eighteenth century, but, as we shall soon see, at that time it was a breath of fresh air.

In the 1950s, it started to assume significant dimensions. In those days, physics dominated the scientific panorama, or at least the imagination of the educated. The discoveries made by physicists revealed that matter is constituted of relatively few elementary particles which combine in many different ways, liberating previously unimaginable sources of energy. It was then that the other sciences, attracted by a paradigm that reduced the complex to the very simple, attempted to find the lowest possible common denominator applicable to their discipline. At the same time, again following the lead of physics, there was a general attempt to compress knowledge into mathematical models. This meant introducing formal analyses, starting from stylized descriptions of each and every phenomenon.

Mathematical models were constructed to represent human behaviour as well as the development of natural events.

When we consider the actions of individuals, whether performed in groups or alone—which is in fact the object of psychology—we have a low-level description of what happens, a level we could almost define as material. This is not the level we normally use when considering everyday life—goals, emotions, actions, thoughts—but it is simplest, as it corresponds to the functioning of our organism, our body.

Looking at the question from this point of view, man (in the sense of human bodies) is without doubt part of nature. This gives substance to the hope that if in the future we are able to conduct a detailed analysis of every part of the human body, we will have a match between the discoveries of experimental psychologists and the results of our investigations of elementary biological mechanisms. Then we will be able to demolish the complexities of daily life behind its myriad appearances, reducing it to an underlying biological reality (whether dealing with heredity, genetics, or the functioning of the brain).

And so the dream from the past would come true: psychology would become part of that mixture of physics and biology which in the modern world provides an explanation of the human body and its natural history. In this light psychology, and probably the social disciplines as well, would at best be 'provisional' sciences. The lexicon of everyday life would be quite another matter altogether; probably we will never be completely rid of that ingenuous psychology formed from descriptions of thoughts, wishes, needs. After all, this is also the language adopted by 'psychological scientists' outside the walls of their laboratories.

The old dream cherished by a number of psychologists of rescuing the mind from the dominion of the scientific lexicon is a very attractive simplification, and is extremely powerful in its general organization. Today, with the evolution of novel sophisticated technologies and the consequent advances made in the realm of mind–brain relationships, it seems within reach once more, so we should not be surprised that it has managed to invade the media and show business in various ways (for example, the recent rash of films about robots).

Summing up, a single language, physics–chemistry and biology, will form the key to revealing the mechanisms of all known phenomena, from the movement of the heavenly bodies to the elementary particles, from the world of nature to the social whirl.

Although this is very attractive in its elegance and simplicity, it is in fact an illusion. It just doesn't work. Why?

Nowadays when everyone has a mobile phone or a computer, or one of these hybrids that are so much the fashion, there is no dearth of examples that explain why reductionism doesn't work.

You need to make a call from a mobile phone. Unfortunately you don't have the instruction manual to hand. You try to conjure up a detailed description of how all the elements that make up the mobile phone function, keeping in mind that they are mostly sand, metals, and plastics (i.e. oil). Would this help you to make that phone call? The fact is that there are various levels of description applicable to machines, artefacts, and organisms, some of which are appropriate for certain purposes but not for others.

If you want to make mobile phones you have to know every single detail of the composite parts of the product. However, if you just want to make a call from a telephone which is already assembled and ready for use, then all you need to know are the basics of its software, which are explained in the instruction manual. This is the level that psychology is now able to explain after a century of study of the 'software' supplied by the process of natural evolution. This software has been laboriously reconstructed, step by step, inventing experiments to supply clues as to how the human mind works. It was, and is, a complex task.

There is of course a significant difference between mobile phones and humans. Man designs and produces mobile phones but he did not design himself. We build robots, claiming that they run on software similar to the human mind, and that we can interact with them through the same programs that determine thoughts and emotions. However, the robotic hardware was constructed by man, manipulating the inert substances of a computer's component parts. Man, on the contrary, is the product of natural evolution, developing almost imperceptibly over millions of years, a fact which makes it difficult to reconstruct his natural history a priori as this would require working backwards. Having said that, however, amazing steps forwards (or should we say backwards?) have been made in recent years using biological techniques. It is like trying to understand what has happened in an epic movie from the final scenes. The beginning and the central part of the plot are lost. Have you seen Ridley Scott's *Blade Runner* (1982), a forerunner of the cyberpunk genre, or Steven Spielberg's *ET* (1982), a film that established a box-office record? The success of these films ought to have facilitated the assimilation of the concept that the 'software' of life is independent of the material of which the living body is composed, but actually they probably produced the opposite effect. In fact, the idea of man as a machine has taken root in the social imagination, based on the concept that even bodies constructed in the most diverse ways can love and be loved.

Cognitive processes: what they are, how they work, and where they are located

Theoretically, in order to study any mental process you need to be able to define what you are examining, how it works, and where its neurophysiological correlates are located. In a nutshell, you have to have the answers to three questions: What?, How?, and Where? Over the last decade light has been brought to bear on the last question: Where?.

As we have seen in the previous chapter, new techniques which seem to photograph the brain at work without damaging it (see the section on cognitive subtraction) have greatly contributed to progress in this field and have promoted a revival of the classic utopia of reducing the mind to the functioning of the brain. This is more than just a passing whim; it reflects true progress.

The French philosopher Julien Offray de La Mettrie, who lived and worked in the 1700s, elaborated a concept of man and animals as being machines (*L'Homme Machine*, his famous work of 1748, originally translated as *Man a Machine*) which has left its mark on post-modern times. Today his 'materialistic' and 'machine' concepts appear plausible because there are only two common-sense options available. Either you embrace the idea that the human mind and the brain are made of different stuff, as Descartes did a century before de La Mettrie (but today this is generally viewed as 'Descartes' error'), or you are forced to assume that when there is mental activity something changes in the brain and/or the rest of the body—in fact, man as a material machine.[1]

If you support de La Mettrie's hypothesis, you are faced with the problem of where cognitive activities are actually located. However, if you prefer Descartes' position, then it is a moot question because the mind is composed of a different substance from the rest of the body (although you will have the problem of how the two are connected, if they are connected—but that is another story).

The fact of the matter is that nowadays not only scientists but also common sense, albeit rather vaguely and ambiguously if the studies conducted on the question are to be believed, embrace de La Mettrie's hypothesis. According to polls conducted in the USA, today only very few psychologists believe that there is something beyond, or maybe we should say above, biology, physics, and chemistry. However, this does not mean that they are all reductionists, accepting only biochemical explanations of the phenomena. On the contrary, these psychologists continue to do their work. They explore animal behaviour at phenomenal and experimental level (we must not forget that man is an animal, after all). They haven't discarded their methodologies which flank these new frontiers that have been opened up by the progress made in our knowledge of the brain.

In other words, psychologists are perfectly content to study the 'higher' level, where emotions, memories, actions, choices, decisions and indecisions, and so on take place. It is the question of how mobile phones and computers work all over again; we can describe how they work 'as if' we were ignorant of the materials of which their component parts are made (the example is equally applicable to washing machines and other 'intelligent' utensils even if they are less 'noble' than the computer).

'As if' is an important stratagem, which was used first by economists. Their investigations of human behaviour are based on the supposition that human actions expose what they call 'revealed preferences'. In theory, the preferences which reveal our tastes (which can be deduced from our behaviour, i.e. our choices) correspond to something which happens in our heads. To be frank, in most cases economists couldn't care less what actually happens in the head, and human thought gets its own back. In fact the economists' idea of how the world works, greatly simplified in order to fit their mathematical models, is at odds with reality. We will return to this point when we discuss 'neuroeconomics'.

However, it must be said that a number of psychologists (particularly those who study aggregate behaviour, i.e. behaviour of more than one person) tended to criticize the turn that things were taking, a trend inspired by the victorious paradigms of the 'hard sciences' and therefore, in their view, reductionist in the biological sense. Here we will cite just one example of the many available. Francesca Emiliani, an Italian social psychologist (social psychologists study groups and communities rather than individuals), attributes what in her opinion is a caricature of human behaviour that leads to the various 'neuro-' reductionisms[2] to contagion by the hard sciences.

At this point a question comes spontaneously to mind. Are we sure that this is a purely academic question between scientists and philosophers, a match to be played out exclusively by these two groups? A recent research study published in the *Journal of Cognitive Neuroscience* by a group of researchers at Yale University opens up new horizons and sows the seed of doubt.

Deena Skolnick Weisberg and other well-known scientists such as Frank Keil, editor of the MIT *Encyclopedia
of the Cognitive Sciences*, collaborated on an ingenious
research project with the object of ascertaining whether
a particular predilection for 'neuro-' explanations has
its roots in the way the general public conceives the
world. Will the general public believe any pseudo-
explanation, as long as it is well presented? And what
exactly does 'well presented' entail?

This group of scholars wanted to know whether
explanations of human behaviour (some correct and
others not) would seem more credible if they were integrated with certain neuroscientific information. With
this purpose in mind they drew up descriptions of psychological mechanisms and enriched them with neuroscientific information regarding cerebral location. They
then investigated the effect that the addition of the neuroscientific information had compared with identical
descriptions without the added information.

One of the phenomena employed was that known
as 'the curse of knowledge', which is the term used to

identify the tendency to overestimate the extent to which a piece of information is known to others if we ourselves are aware of it. The 'curse' is the fact that we are condemned to project our knowledge onto others, which results in our becoming egocentric.[4] The Yale researchers described the phenomenon in the following terms.

The researchers created a list of facts that about 50 per cent of people knew. Subjects in this experiment read the list of facts and had to say which ones they knew. They then had to judge what percentage of other people would know those facts. The researchers found that the subjects responded differently about other people's knowledge of a fact when the subjects themselves knew that fact. If the subjects knew a fact, they said that an inaccurately large percentage of others would also know it. For example, if a subject already knew that Hartford was the capital of Connecticut, that subject might say that 80 per cent of people would know this, even though the correct answer is 50 per cent. The researchers called this finding 'the curse of knowledge'.

After having described the phenomenon, the researchers drew up four types of explanation.

a) Good explanation without neuroscience (<u>underlined</u>).

b) Bad explanation without neuroscience (*italics*).

c) Good explanation (<u>underlined</u>) with neuroscience (**bold**).

d) Bad explanation (*italics*) with neuroscience (**bold**).

The good (<u>underlined</u>) and bad (*italics*) explanations without the neuroscientific addition are:

- This curse happens because <u>subjects have trouble switching their point of view to consider what someone else might know, mistakenly projecting their own knowledge onto others.</u>

- This 'curse' happens because *subjects make more mistakes when they have to judge the knowledge of others. People are much better at judging what they themselves know.*

And now the good explanation (<u>underlined</u>) and the bad explanation (*italics*) preceded in both cases by the neuroscientific information (**bold**):

- **Brain scans** indicate that the 'curse' happens because **of the frontal lobe brain circuitry known to be involved in**

self-knowledge. <u>Subjects have trouble switching their point</u> <u>of view to consider what someone else might know, mistakenly</u> <u>projecting their own knowledge onto others.</u>

- **Brain scans** indicate that this 'curse' happens because **of the frontal lobe brain circuitry known to be involved in self-knowledge**. *Subjects make more mistakes when they have to judge the knowledge of others. People are much better at judging what they themselves know.*

The good and bad explanations and the integration of neuroscientific information were combined to produce the four types of explanation reported above. Then two sample groups were selected from a given population. One sample group was given the description of the phenomenon and the two explanations, one good and one bad, without the neuroscientific addition; the other group received the same description and the same two explanations, one good and one bad, but with the addition of the neuroscientific information.

The curse of knowledge phenomenon together with 17 other similar effects, all accompanied by the four types of explanation, were presented to two samples of 40 people extracted from the same population. In all cases the neuroscientific addition was an indication to the effect that a particular area of the brain was involved. The neuroscientific addition was always identical for both good and bad explanations. These latter were merely reaffirmations of the psychological effect, phrased differently; in other words, they were circular pseudo-explanations.

The task required the participants to rate the explanation, using a seven-point scale with zero as the neutral midpoint and ranging from −3 (very unsatisfactory) to +3 (very satisfactory). Before starting the experiment, the participants were told that the psychological effect of the explanations which they would be asked to evaluate had been demonstrated experimentally and were solid, having been repeated several times.

The results found by the Yale researchers were extremely interesting. No differences emerged between men and women, or among the 18 psychological effects used. The good explanations were considered to be more satisfactory than the bad; moreover, the good explanations with the neuroscientific addition were on average just as satisfactory as those without. The finding of particular interest was that the bad explanations with the neuroscientific addition were considered to be much more satisfacory than the bad explanations without the addition.

In summary:

1. The participants were presented with a description of an experimentally ascertained psychological effect which had been reported in the literature.

2. The bad explanation of the effect was simply a reformulation of its description: i.e. a circular explanation phrased differently, but coinciding to all intents and purposes with the original description.

3. The addition of the neuroscientific information (the cerebral location of the phenomenon) magically rendered the bad explanation satisfactory, at least for non-experts.

The Yale researchers did not stop there; they wanted to know what would happen if the sample was extended to 22 students attending an introductory level cognitive neuroscience course. They found that the results did not change, even though the students were more familiar with neuroscience than the participants in the first study. At this point Weisberg and her colleagues tested another 48 people who had finished their training in neuroscience. The results in this case were crucial. The experts did not fall into the trap! They were able to distinguish the good explanations from the bad explanations, independently of the addition of the neuroscientific information. This result is particularly relevant because it shows that only experts are immune to this form of deception. All the others, in practice the vast majority of the population, are taken in by the addition of neuroscientific information (in itself correct) which makes all the difference between a credible explanation and an explanation considered to be unsatisfactory.

In other words, the bad explanation becomes credible when integrated with neuroscience which has, so to speak, powers of redemption. The general public tends to misunderstand the addition of neuroscience which, as a consequence, has the power to transform an unsatisfactory explanation into a satisfactory one. Put bluntly, the neuroscientific information provides added value that converts an erroneous explanation into a credible explanation.

This certainly provides food for thought. It is insidious—when we discuss matters that are ethically sensitive the addition of a biological justification can transform a position which otherwise would not be tenable into being acceptable. When discussions regarding the body are mixed with discussions about the mind, the body comes to the foreground and the mind slips into the background. Even if the explanations given in mental terms are simply a rephrased description of the phenomenon, i.e. circular explanations, this is not apparent if neuroscientific terms are added.

All non-experts tend to fall into this trap. We shall see later how this tendency to cling to the conditions of the body can produce dramatic effects when decisions regarding the body are of a ideological–political nature (life, death, copulation, abortion, bringing up children, and so on).

To sum up, the findings of the Yale research group highlight a general ingenuous representation of the mind–brain relationship shared by non-experts. The general public is inclined to accept a form of 'medico-biological' supremacy in the description of psychological phenomena.

The nature of the seductive allure of neuroscience explanations

The experiment conducted by the Yale researchers is extremely astute in demonstrating the persuasive impact of references to cerebral locations. It is almost as if evoking a part of the body affected by a psychological condition is more important than the description of the condition itself. Of course, this trick only works with non-experts and consequently increases the burden of responsibility that falls on the few who are well versed in the discipline. There have already been cases of this.

The front page of the *New York Times* of 11 November 2007 carried an article with the headline 'This is your brain on politics'. It described an experiment conducted by Marco Iacoboni and his colleagues with 20 volunteers, 10 men and 10 women, who had stated that they did not know for whom they would vote in the forthcoming US presidential primary elections. Iacoboni and his colleagues mapped the cerebral activity of these volunteers while they looked at politically related words (such as Democrat, Republican, etc.) and photographs of candidates, and watched video extracts of the candidates' speeches.

The publication of this article was met with a volley of protest and criticisms from various quarters.[5] Russell Poldrack, who at the time was teaching at the University of California where Iacoboni himself works, and 16 other well-known neuroscientists published a letter of protest three days later in the same newspaper, denying that it is possible to infer particular mental states through activation of specific cerebral areas by the means claimed by Iacoboni. Elizabeth Phelps, a neuroscientist at New York University and one of the co-signers of the protest letter, stated that while it is correct that the amygdala is affected by a state of anxiety, the same holds true for strong odours, sexually stimulating images, and so on. It is both rash and misleading to claim, on these grounds alone, that a candidate like Mitt Romney throws the electorate into a state of anxiety.

The scientific point under attack here is the demonstration of the strength of the 'cerebral state–mental state' connection. Iacoboni claimed that it is correct to use this connection in probabilistic terms, with which Poldrack agreed in principle.[6] Poldrack's objection was that data on probability are not yet decisive and do not indicate matching correspondences. As an example, an investigation published on PubMed on 3 June 2008 indicated 88 responses for 'amygdala AND happiness', 585 responses for 'amygdala AND reward', and 1314 responses for 'amygdala AND anxiety'. This all goes to show that it is not possible to establish a triple correspondence between an emotion, the activation of a cerebral area such as the amygdala, and a photograph of a candidate for the US presidential primary election, Mitt Romney.

In the previous chapter we have seen the traps that lie in ambush along this particular path, in the sense that we are not dealing with one-to-one correspondences here. Moreover, the article in the *New York Times* stated that the 20 volunteers were particularly little affected by pictures of Barack Obama and John McCain, the eventual presidential candidates.

The debate over this article, which became very heated in the US media, from scientific journals to the popular press, and to newspapers and television, included both banal and stimulating aspects.

The accusation (however valid) that Iacoboni's co-authors were involved in a form of conflict of interest as they worked for FKF Applied Research, a private company based in Washington, DC, which sells brain-mapping studies to major companies with a particular focus on the efficacy of advertising messages, was banal.

Less banal, though certainly not new, was the irritation expressed by the scientists at those journalists whose aim is to produce a scoop, while neglecting to ensure that the information they are transmitting is correct. In contemporary journalism a certain dose of Marinism (the term is coined from the name of the Neapolitan poet, Giambattista Marino (1569–1625) who wrote *è del poeta il fin la meraviglia* [the poet's aim, marvel must be]) is always, and legitimately, present.

This episode is part of the thorny debate involving serious scientific journalism and journalism for purely commercial purposes which simply aims at titillating the public to attract readers or 'spectators' (to whom to sell advertising space, paid for as a function of the size of the audience).

Rather more interesting is the accusation that the illustrations accompanying the article (which is basically well written) are sections and photographs of the brain. Such illustrations tend to fascinate the public as the brain has been shrouded in mystery for years. It has been seen as a sort of 'black box' that can only be accessed when no longer of use, when its owner is dead (see the discussion of Paul Broca's work at the beginning of Chapter I).

These press scenarios involve us in a sort of postmodern *Wunderkammer*, the cabinets of curiosities that were the forerunners of today's museums and influenced many contemporaneous works of art. They were very popular in Europe in the sixteenth century, and their popularity peaked in the baroque period of the seventeenth century and continued into the eighteenth century, stimulated by the love of scientific curiosities that characterized that century. The cabinets of curiosities overflowed with naturalia, freaks of nature such as animals with two heads, rare or unknown fish and birds, and fruit and vegetables of unusual dimensions.

The sense of wonder evoked by these articles in the press is similar to that aroused by the eighteenth-century cabinets of curiosities. It follows from the nineteenth-century tradition of scientific and technological wonders which today have pride of place in science museums. For example, when electricity took the fancy of the general public at the end of the nineteenth century as a phenomenon, it was used as a 'metaphor' for psychodiagnosis and psychotherapeutic purposes. Hence the popularity of mesmerism, from the name of Franz Anton Mesmer (1734–1815) who invented 'animal magnetism', which became so fashionable that it was even mentioned in Mozart's opera *Così fan Tutte*. In the first act, Ferrando and Guglielmo, the lovers of Dorabella and Fiordiligi, respectively, feign death from love and are 'resuscitated' by Despina, the maid, dressed as a doctor, who restores them to life with an enormous magnet:

Questo è quel pezzo	This is
Di calamita:	A piece of magnet,
Pietra mesmerica,	The stone which the great
Ch'ebbe l'origine	Doctor Mesmer discovered
Nell'Alemagna	In Germany
Che poi si celebre	And then became
Là in Francia fu	So famous in France.

When electricity became accepted as a form of energy, mesmerism transformed into spiritualism and clinical therapies, which were enhanced by man-made technology, similarly to brain scans. Electricity, in all its mystery, was raised to therapeutic purposes, with results that appeared to be little less than miraculous. A more recent example is the Higgs boson: to justify the astronomical costs of the experiment launched in Switzerland in 2009 to European tax payers, the media reported that the objective is to photograph the 'God particle' and thus reveal the origins of the universe to all. Again, attention is attracted by the 'marvel' mechanism—the awesome prospect of the discovery of unknown realities, unknown because they are invisible. This simple mechanism, which is the basis of those geographical discoveries that always enthralled us in childhood, never fails to work.

Here two aspects should be kept separate, to avoid confusion. On the one hand, we have the genuine scientific aspects of technology, which are astounding in their own right because of their inherent innovation and the fact that they break with past tradition, as in the case of electricity, and fMRI today. On the other hand, the awe and amazement generated by these innovations encourage a rather too casual and often misleading use of such discoveries, in true Marinistic style. We have already seen how today's sophisticated equipment, whose functioning is shrouded in mystery for most people, can film a part of the human body that was previously totally unknown and associate it with the origins of our cognitive states.

The brain at work and the supremacy of the body

We now come to what is probably the most interesting point of the issue: multi-stability, one of the most general laws of psychology.

When a part of the body acquires particular relevance and comes into the foreground, all the rest fades into the background. If we want to predict how swing voters will cast their votes, we start from the brain, and not vice versa. In other words, the activity detected by the scanner shows (or, more precisely, convinces us that we have seen) something of which we were not aware, that is outside the boundaries of our knowledge, as in the effect of the advertising examined by FKF Applied Research. This is a strong essential component of the appeal exerted by fMRI. This is the origin, and the roots, of the 'wonder' effect of the press's cabinet of curiosities.

The other important point is the possibility of a simple, direct, and apparently scientific explanation of complex phenomena. Once the discovery of a one-to-one connection between a cognitive state and the activation of an area of the brain has been disseminated, the phenomenon has been revealed and the problem has apparently been solved. Single-cause explanations, where an effect is produced by a single cause, are the most effective and 'credible'.[7]

However, the divide between scoop journalism and serious research is not quite so clear cut. This 'grey area' is one of the most dangerous consequences of ill-judged scientific publications in the popular press and was one of the principal points raised by the neuroscientists in the debate following the publication of the article in the *New York Times* (a debate which was picked up by a number of other newspapers, both inside and outside the USA). It lies at the roots of new alleged disciplines, in which traditional studies are revitalized by the addition of the 'neuro-' prefix, generating new areas of study, or rather what are presumed to be new areas of study. As we shall see, these are nebulous cases where it is not always easy to discern between positive and misleading contributions induced by the use of these new technologies.

In general, the most positive aspect of the debate in the press regarding the various 'neurodisciplines' is the propagation of the idea that humans have evolved in such a way as to be 'made like that'. Fortunately, this has ousted a concept that was popular in 1968—the idea that everything was 'socially constructed'. Time and time again sociology professors of the day proclaimed that we reflect the society and the culture in which we live (when the young Legrenzi, not yet a professor, dared to cast a shadow of doubt on this unshakeable belief, he was howled down by a young lady with these words, 'So young, but already a slave of capitalism!').

Forty years later the dedicated scholar Giovanni Jervis wrote of the prototype of the anti-psychiatrist, an important figure of the 1960s:

if there was no bad social interference our mind would be acceptably healthy and happy. In this way we are convinced that all that is evil is always somewhere else, and that the problems [we encounter] have their origins in the prejudices of a middle class society or the intrigues of doctors and biologists.

He concluded that this line of thought is on its way to extinction. Sadly, the pendulum ended its oscillations on the opposite side, less blustery and rhetorical perhaps, but much more insidious because of this.

These then are the excesses of the recent past which, contrasted with the discoveries of our times, make it even more impressive that not only do we now know that humans have bodies, which of course is obvious, but we are starting to find out how the mind–body connection functions, about which so much has been said since Descartes. In other words, the various neuro-disciplines play a positive role in demonstrating that not everything is the fruit of learning and of our biography (and the social environment).

We like to think of ourselves in this light as beings who are not just the exclusive product of our particular lives, and therefore of the specific environment in which we were brought up. Following the discovery of genetics, we no longer believe the myth that man comes into the world as a blank page, and his character is then written by society and the culture in which he happens to live. And in a way this knowledge liberates us a little. All the same, the understandable enthusiasm for these wonderful and sometimes astounding discoveries in the field of neuroscience is not always put to the best use. On the contrary, sometimes it is used to legitimize pure and simple mystification.

In examining the new neurodisciplines we have adopted an implicit hierarchy, starting from the more reputable research, then progressing to those which serve as a support for the others, and terminating with those which are exclusively 'advertising'.

The most reputable of all is of course neuroscience, but we have already discussed this field of study, which is uncontaminated by mystification and only sporadically a victim of scoop journalism, in the Chapter I.

Neuroeconomy

Psychologists have dedicated years of study to human behaviour in the area of economics, and have encountered systematic violations of what the economists define as 'rational behaviour', many of which are not just of theoretical interest, but have profound implications regarding the choices people make in savings, consumption, and pension plans, and, last but not least, how they invest their savings (or increasingly often, how bankers instruct them to invest their savings). Many years ago economists tried to defend their theoretical models by sustaining that these violations depended on ignorance, lack of experience, poor training, and sometimes bad faith—problems that could easily be corrected. However, faced with concrete experimental evidence and, most importantly, in the light of human behaviour world-wide, they were forced to renounce their defence theories. And this is where neuroeconomy comes into play.

Neuroeconomic mechanisms cannot be modified because they depend on how the mind processes information and makes its choices without our being aware of it. The fact that this processing happens without our being aware it is attributed to the automatic systems which are triggered by the functioning of the brain, and which remain unchanged (unless we consider natural changes brought about by the evolution of the human species which require millions of years to perfect). A number of examples illuminate the profound practical implications that this has, but for the purposes of this book we shall describe the relationships between the perception of risk, the passage of time, and gratification.

Beliefs being equal, people are considerably influenced by circumstances and therefore appear to be changeable. Moreover, in order to be completely sure that they have understood the scenario in which they have to operate, they seek confirmation of their decisions from many quarters. Unfortunately, what the human mind considers to be an adequate number of confirmations is quite often excessive in today's world (with the result that decisions are made too late).

The combined effect of these two mechanisms is disastrous when people, believing themselves to be experts, decide to invest their savings personally, playing the financial markets on the basis of their own evaluations of the most favourable circumstances. If these decisions were to depend on automatic cerebral mechanisms, which were unknown to us, it would be extremely difficult to modify such self-destructive behaviour.

Neuroeconomic models can also explain why two apparently different phenomena are governed by the same mechanism or, vice versa, why two apparently similar phenomena have different neural correlates. This became clear when the neural circuit of gratification was fully understood.

Time is a crucial factor in psychoeconomy. Possibly stemming back to the origins of man as a hunter–gatherer, the human brain is constructed in such a way as to register short-term gratification and pain. However, our contemporary existence requires much longer lead times, not only to manage savings, but also for study and work, obliging us to delay gratification. We are well aware of this, but sometimes we fall into temptation not just once, but over and over again, even if we have experienced and are fully conscious of the negative effects of our failure to persevere. Here, an understanding of the neural circuit of gratification can be extremely illuminating.

It must be said, out of intellectual honesty, that neuroeconomy is very fashionable.[8] Frequently the enthusiasm of the supporters of this new field of research leads them to reformulate what is already acquired knowledge thanks to the experiments conducted by psychologists, simply by substituting 'mind' by 'brain', and believing that in doing so they have enriched the reputation of this field of study. In cases such as these, we fall victim to the effect that the Yale scholars analysed so well, in which the addition of neuroscientific information improves an explanation. And the easiest way to do this, of course, is to substitute 'mind' by 'brain'.

Neuromarketing and neurodesign

The term 'neuromarketing' can be used to indicate two different things. It can be an attempt, which is sometimes successful, to apply what we know about the neural correlates of decisions and emotions to traditional marketing techniques, which are then given new names. In this case, the 'neuro-' prefix is used to enhance the time-proven techniques of marketing, and of the psychology of sales and advertising communication.

The basic idea is that the different parts of the brain function in different ways and therefore we have to create different advertising messages and sales mechanisms depending on which neural circuit we want to activate. Fundamentally, what is being presented as a great novelty is often nothing more than another 'innovative' sales technique to re-propose a well-tested marketing package. Given that the clients purchasing the package can be compared to the non-experts in the research carried out at Yale, it will come as no surprise that the addition of a neuroscientific component attracts and convinces the management of the client company to seek out consultants offering these packages. What it amounts to is that tried and tested formulas are trotted out with a new look, and apparently 'offer more guarantees and are more effective' because they are 'more scientific'.

There is also a serious aspect in that the issue is frequently confused by the use of the same label. In this case the terms 'neuro-' and 'neuromarketing' are not used in relation to the human brain, but to a form of artificial intelligence which duplicates human behaviour and the purchasing and consumer patterns of the public.

Many years ago, one of the authors (Paolo Legrenzi) acted as consultant to a well-known industrialist whose hobby was observing housewives and their shopping trolleys at his supermarket checkouts. He was simply doing in his head what supermarkets today carry out using dedicated software—processing statistics of who buys what, what is bought, and how it is bought (combined with which other products).

Nowadays, given that people tend to pay mostly using credit cards or something similar, this can be done on the basis of individual customer data rather than by point-of-sale observation, defining a potential customer as the result of his/her subsequent choices. This is done by breaking down an individual's data and reconstructing his/her consumer–saver brain from his/her choices recorded in different places at different points in time. This technique is known as data fusion, and the data obtained can be used time and time again to construct consumer or customer prototypes.

The term 'data fusion' originated in 1984 when Lockheed Martin researchers published two studies on the possibility of correlating and fusing data from various sources: an individual's emails (which at that time were not as common as they are now) and all their other databases as well as the payment systems adopted. A.C. Nielsen, a world leader in marketing and advisory services, then developed data fusion systems for consumer segmentation and for the identification of consumer trends from a small number of pointers and faint signals. Unsurprisingly, neuromarketing met with strong opposition, given its vaguely Orwellian overtones—the fact that we are spied on without our knowledge or consent by agencies interested in our behaviour (but today's techniques go well beyond those of the famous novel 1984, which was based on primitive technologies). However, data fusion can also be used to defend the consumer. For example, the analysis conducted by John Poindexter and Robert Popp of the Defence Advanced Research Projects Agency (DARPA) in the USA showed that the attacks on the World Trade Centre in 1993 and in Oklahoma City in 1995 could have been avoided if the government had checked the commercial database of purchases of fertilizer by individuals not involved in agriculture.

There are also subsectors of neuromarketing, for example neurodesign, which Donald Norman calls emotional design. These are variations on the theme we discussed at the beginning of this chapter; when designing an object or a representation, these designers look beyond its merely functional aspects and take into consideration the emotions it will evoke in the user. Then they add a few notions regarding the neural basis of the emotions, shake up their ingredients, and the cocktail is ready to serve.

If by the term 'neuromarketing' we mean all the aspects discussed above, and not just the 'repackaging' operations, then, passing fashions apart, it will not be easy to shrug off the problem.[9]

Neuroaesthetics, neuroethics, and neurotheology

Here three traditional fields of knowledge have been spruced up and their old philosophical themes reworked into new formats. These allegedly new disciplines have a similar starting point. What happens inside our heads when we pray or experience art? Psychologists have been investigating these questions for decades and have offered a range of different answers (remember Mosso and Farmer Bertino?). Apparently the answer to 'where' has now been found—the 'where' in our body.

Neuroaesthetics started with the work of Semir Zeki, Professor of Neurobiology at University College London, who explored what happens in our brains when we observe works of art. The criticism that can be made of this concept is similar to that which was raised when the principles of perceptive organization were applied to the observation of works of art, as Rudolf Arnheim did in a number of classic works. The point is that these principles, and the cortical areas involved, function in the same way when exposed to any visual stimulus, whether it is artistic or not, and to any emotion, no matter whether it is triggered by a work of art or by another form of input.

In other words, the approach claims to explain the experience of art, but does not analyse the specifics of the experience.

The neurophysiological discovery of empathy, the capacity of putting oneself in someone else's shoes, appears be more directly related to artistic and ethical issues.

As discussed in Chapter I, in the mid-1990s Giacomo Rizzolatti and a group of researchers at the University of Parma discovered the presence of mirror neurons, a particular type of neuron which is present in certain areas of the parietal and frontal lobes of the macaque. The functioning of these neurons, on which we dwelt at length, should be considered as a prerequisite for artistic emotion and ethical judgement. However, once again the specifics of the artistic and moral judgements are not considered, although we could consider this discovery as a precondition for these types of judgement. These preconditions, which correspond to neuronal circuits common to the entire human species, would constitute a sort of universal grammar limiting the number of ethical and aesthetic judgements it is possible to make.

As in the case of the universal linguistic grammars introduced by Chomsky, we would have grammars constraining perception and emotion. Therefore, however strong the impact of circumstances and culture might be, there would be boundaries and limitations clearly defined by the way the human brain functions.

The contributions of these disciplines are interesting in so far as they demonstrate that not all theoretically possible aesthetic and ethical judgements are psychologically plausible and performable in cognitive terms.

A similar reasoning is applicable to neurotheology. As man conceives of God in various different ways and circumstances, there must be a common prerequisite, a neuronal prerequisite, for this concept in which the various religions have their roots. The issue here is rather more complex than in the previous cases as it is extremely difficult to find the lowest common denominator for all religious beliefs. To be precise, common denominators exist, but they are far removed from the specifics of the various religions. In simpler terms, humans are constructed to believe and babies are born with an innate capacity for belief. This is undoubtedly a true story, but it is a different story; it has already been told and its explanation does not need the support of a 'neuro' component.[10]

Neuropolitics

During World Brain Awareness Week in 2008 a convention on neuropolitics was held at the Faculty of Psychology, La Sapienza University, Rome, under the patronage of the Neuroscience Laboratory. What was on the agenda? The speakers touched on various subjects: those who came closest to neuropolitics focused on the neurocognitive correlates of liberal and conservative behaviour and political choices that can be explained in the light of the possibility of 'showing' the various brain areas involved.

We have already dealt with this point in our discussion of the debate provoked by the *New York Times* article describing Marco Iacoboni's research study, but it is worth returning to this case because it demonstrates that the attraction of the neuro-disciplines is not just a passing fad, blown up by the media and a rather slapdash popular scientific press (remember … the heart of the future is firmly rooted in the past!).

On 19 September 2008 the extremely reputable journal *Science*—the same journal which in June 2008 contained the scientific debate triggered by Iacoboni's research—published an article with a curious title, 'Political attitudes vary with physiological traits'.[11] What was this research about? The authors found that a sample of 46 people with strong political beliefs reacted differently to a series of sudden disruptive noises and threatening visual images. The subjects with a higher resistance to these disturbances had less accentuated physiological reactions and were in favour of foreign aid, liberal immigration policies, and so on. A simple correlation, which is in no way surprising, is that the more fearful of the participants were less well disposed to those in need. However, this research was presented within the sphere of traditional research according to which 'political beliefs can be predicted by observing brain activation patterns'. In the abstract, the authors conclude that 'although political views have been thought to arise largely from individuals' experiences, recent research suggests that they may have a biological basis.' What exactly does this mean? Either it means something extremely obvious, or something completely wrong.

It is evident that any attitude or thought has a biological base, and that nowadays supporters of the Cartesian theory that the mind and the brain are two different substances are few and far between. However, it is misleading to state that a person makes specific political choices because his/her brain has a particular configuration. And this is what these researchers seem to be saying in the abstract published in *Science* although, to be fair, they are more cautious in the body of the article itself and in the conclusions. They advance the hypothesis that their data do not go beyond correlations between variables and that it is 'More likely is that physiological responses to generic threats and political attitudes on policies related to protecting the social order may both derive from a common source'. But what is this common source? In the conclusion, the authors suggest that this might be the amygdala, which we have discussed above.

If this is really the case, the reader could easily reach the conclusion (not supported by data) that the functioning of the amygdala when faced with threatening situations explains different political leanings. Of course, this is an erroneous conclusion because correlation is not always causality.[12] Psychologists of thinking have taught us that common sense confuses these two types of relation, and that if two things are usually found in tandem we tend to assume that one causes the other (which in fact is often the case).

Once again, the public can be misled by this recourse to the well-known difficulty in distinguishing correlation from causality, and the appeal exerted by the brain. And, as noted earlier, this article appeared in a highly reputable scientific journal.[13] Just imagine what will happen when results of this type are simplified for the popular press!

CONCLUSIONS

Is there a moral to this story? We could easily dismiss it as a passing whim, a fashion blown out of proportion by the media, as happened in the case of electricity and anti-psychiatry.

The popular scientific press could hardly believe its luck in finding a new appealing story to recount, triggered by the discovery of the 'visibility' of the neuron-psyche connection, rather similar to what happened with the famous Northwest Passage, the channel that connects the oceans above Canada, when the melting of the polar cap in 2010 rendered it navigable for the first time. Now another passage is being explored, the passage that connects the brain to the mind, which is rendered accessible by the new technologies that we are told can film cerebral activity. This is one approach, but there is another interpretation possible, less ephemeral and more disturbing. And a number of clues point in this direction.

One of the authors, Paolo Legrenzi, has started to repeat the experiment originally conducted by the Yale University researchers to try to understand why the addition of a neuroscientific component makes something credible when in fact it is not. The qualitative responses, although they have no scientific value, suggest an interpretation. It can be assumed that the power of conviction that the neuroscientific component exerts on non-experts is to be found in a functional, rather than a materialist, interpretation. In other words, what convinces is not so much the fact that a part of the brain is mentioned, but that the neuroscientific element provides the possibility of identifying the precise cause of the functioning or malfunctioning of a cognitive mechanism. When your car breaks down, knowing what part of the engine has caused the problem is the first step towards having it repaired. Similarly, knowing which part of the brain is 'responsible' is key to understanding the cause of the cognitive phenomenon as well as the functioning of the brain itself. The process starts from the brain and proceeds to the mind, not vice versa.

This approach to dealing with cognitive problems, starting from the brain, and hence from the body, not only overturns the philosophy of the 1960s (everything is cultural as it has been socially constructed) but also forms part of a wider movement which, according to the philosopher Giorgio Agamben, characterizes contemporaneity. Agamben takes as his starting point the declaration that technological progress has blurred the borders of body-related phenomena and, in so doing, has decreed its centrality. In fact, events which were once established by nature are now decided by man. If life and death are no longer natural, but defined and limited on the basis of political and ideological choices, then it is crucial to define the body and how it works. In other words, these definitions depend on the preferences, or the leanings, of an authority, whether it be the church, the state, or science (more precisely, medicine, as personified by doctors and researchers).

When it is possible to modify something, we have to know what exactly it is that we are modifying. This is the cognitive criterion for establishing what is under our control (i.e. we control what is modifiable).

There have been a number of notorious cases recently that have been widely discussed in the press and have highlighted the following questions. When exactly does life commence? When does life cease to be? It is easy to demonstrate that it is that part of the body known as the brain which plays a role in today's definitions of life and death.[1] If the power to feel pain and emotion is already developed in the fetus, and is triggered by abortion, the mother–child cost–benefit ratio has to be redefined. Can we really define the issue of abortion in terms of a hedonistic cost–benefit equilibrium, a trade-off which involves subjects with very different powers of control over the situation?

The answer to these questions is of vital importance. But over and above the answer that we may decide to give, the world changed radically and for ever as soon as it became feasible to formulate them. Technology has made it possible to substitute a diseased organ with a healthy body part, donated by another person after death. However, if the boundary between life and death is not well defined, there is a significant risk of committing murder. In fact, the difference between murder and a noble gesture is based on the answer to a thorny question. Was the person really dead?

There are various ways of dealing with these issues. According to the traditional Cartesian mind–body dichotomy, the focus is on the body. It is the body that suffers, that thinks, that decides.

This is the essence of the ethical issue underlying the plots of films and books that have dealt with this subject. Sometimes the character who decides to terminate an essential corporeal function, such as respiration, is portrayed as the 'good guy'. In films such as

Million Dollar Baby and *Les Invasions Barbares* (*The Barbarian Invasions*), it is the hero who makes a particular effort to hasten or facilitate death. Here the issue moves into the no-man's land between 'letting/helping a person die' and 'bringing about their death'. The divide here is established by how we perceive the body—in this specific case by how we perceive the functioning of the brain (in fact, the term used as a legal indicator of death is brain death).

Today we are faced with issues of an ethical–political nature, many of which did not arise in the past simply because nature took care of them. Never before has the distinction between 'bare life' (from the Greek ζωή: zoê), the biological life form common to all, and a life specific to an individual possessed such dramatic overtones.[2] The distinction is not always so dramatic, however. In sport, for example, there is the question of the distinction between taking medicine and (ab)using drugs. In aesthetics, should we really try to improve our appearance (in an attempt to increase our power of attraction) by using medical technology such as plastic surgery to change our body? To what extent can we change our corporeal identity before we cease to be ourselves? We can boost our sensations and cognitive capacity with medicines and drugs, but where is the divide between 'in care' and 'doped'?

Faced with these thorny issues, the temptation is to return to the past, to the mind–body dichotomy in which the body was the privileged system of reference. The traditional concept consists in basing the rules of intervention on the biological conditions of the body and making exceptions only in particular cases for humane reasons. However, adopting such a concept now, with the advanced technology available today, could be both dangerous and misleading.

Nothing could be more obvious than having recourse to discoveries in the field of genetics to define the point in which a fetus becomes a person; biological terms define when a person is no longer a person but just a body. However, if we choose to do this, we are totally unaware of the devastating consequences of what we have decided to take for granted.

There is nothing to stop us adopting the opposite approach and assuming that the criteria should be the physical and psychical well-being of the person which, when combined, result in an overall state of well-being. This is quite a significant difference, when all is said and done. In this case, well-being is to the fore, while the body is in the background.

If well-being is taken as the criterion, then it could be assumed that everyone will donate their organs after death. On the contrary, if the body is taken as the criterion, formal consent is needed for the removal of the organs after death. The practical consequences of what we take for granted, in similar cultures in which similar beliefs are practised, are dramatic.[3] For example, the difference between the percentage of organ donors in Austria, where well-being is the criterion, and Germany, where the criterion is the body, is about 90 per cent.

Taking the condition of the body as the basis for defending a person's rights can sometimes produce paradoxical results and be counter-productive. Probably the best-known instances of this are to be found in the choices of the Roman Catholic Church which, concerned by developments in technology, tends (albeit unwittingly) to turn its back on the ancient tenets of wisdom based on charity and solidarity. It goes without saying that we are talking of choices made totally without malice aforethought, as is always the case when a default mechanism takes over. The issue lies in the fact that the Church adopts a bare definition of corporeal conditions as its prime guideline for decision-making. It then has to sustain its position in the opposition camp, which of course has an easy task demonstrating that more lives are lost and more people suffer if the Church refuses to change its stance.

An example of this is to be found in the contrasting positions taken by Giuseppe Remuzzi of the Mario Negri Pharmacological Research Institute and the *Osservatore Romano* (the semi-official newspaper of the Holy See). Writing in Italy's leading financial daily *Il Sole 24 Ore*, 6 September 2008, Remuzzi declared that 'donating organs after death to those in need should be a duty, just like caring for the elderly and vaccinating children'. In an article which appeared on 3 September 2008, the *Osservatore Romano* quoted from a speech made by Pope Benedict XVI many years previously: 'those who fall into an irreversible coma following illness or accident will often be put to death to furnish a supply of organs for transplants'. Remuzzi retorted that such a thing had never happened in the reanimation departments of Italian hospitals.

According to Remuzzi, the consequence of this stand (in which the state of the body and not the overall wellbeing of the person is taken for granted as being the most important element) is that 'someone who could have been a donor of organs, won't be. For every donor lost, two people will have to remain on dialysis, a patient with a heart condition will die, there will be no more hope for an adult and a child waiting for a liver transplant'.

Far be it from us to go into the merits of the medical and nursing aspects of the issue. We simply wish to reflect on the link between the appeal of neuroscientific explanations and the stand that the Catholic Church takes on the issue.[4] In both cases it is the state of the body (and frequently the brain, where death is concerned) that dictates the criteria, whether they be right or wrong. Overall well-being, to which in theory the charity and solidarity of the Church should aspire and to which Remuzzi was referring, remains in the background.

A frequently asked question is why the Catholic Church, which has always professed charity and solidarity, has forced itself, so to speak, to take what appear to the majority to be cruel decisions. This is certainly the case when only the corporeal state is taken into consideration, ignoring the mental functions of the person involved. And it is particularly true when taking decisions involving life, death, upbringing (parents' gender), and, last but not least, medical treatment.

These difficult and complex questions let loose mysteries that develop into problems when we reflect on the allure of the solutions deriving from bringing the brain and body into the foreground. Only profound contemplation of the issues described above will prevent us from losing our way in the maze that technology has created for us. Man, after all, is more than just a body, a bare life.

NOTES

I

At the origins of the mind–brain relationship

1. For further reading in neuroanatomy, see Pinel, P.J., *Psychobiology* (6th edn), Boston, MA: Allyn & Bacon, 2006; Brodal, A., *Neurological Anatomy*, New York: Oxford University Press, 1981. For further reading on language disorders, see Hillis, A., *The Handbook of Adult Language Disorders*. New York: Psychology Press, 2002; Stemmer, B. and Whitaker, H. (eds), *Handbook of Neurolinguistics*, New York: Academic Press, 1998.

2. Fodor, J.A., *Modularity of Mind*, Cambridge, MA: MIT Press, 1983. See also Schlosser, G. and Wagner, G., *Modularity in Development and Evolution*, Chicago, IL: University of Chicago Press, 2004.

NOTES

3. For further reading on Gall's phrenology, see Simpson, D., Phrenology and the neurosciences: contributions of F.J. Gall and J.G. Spurzheim, *ANZ Journal of Surgery*, **75**: 475–82, 2005.

4. Hedlin, J., Mass function and equipotentiality: a reanalysis of Lashley's retention data, *Psychological Reports*, **27**: 899–902, 1970; Orbach, J., *The Neuropsychological Theories of Lashley and Hebb*, New York: University Press of America, 1998.

5. Kanizsa, G., *Organization of Vision*, New York: Praeger, 1979.

6. Freud, S., *Project for a Scientific Psychology* (2nd edn), London: Hogarth Press 1955 (originally written in German in 1895); Freud, S., *On Aphasia: A Critical Study* (transl. E. Stengel), New York: International Universities Press, 1953 (originally published in German in 1891).

7. Teuber, H.L., Physiological psychology, *Annual Review of Psychology*, **6**: 267–96, 1955; Geschwind, N., Disconnection syndromes in animals and man, *Brain*, **88**: 237–94, 585–644, 1965.

8. Mosso's contributions are summarized in Posner, M.I. and Raichle, M.E., *Images of Mind*, New York: Scientific American Library, 1994. The original articles can be read in Mosso, A., Introduzione ad una serie di esperienze sui movimenti del cervello nell' uomo, *Archivio di Scienze Mediche*, **13**: 245–78, 1876; Mosso, A., Sulla circolazione del sangue nel cervello umano, *Memorie della Reale Accademia Nazionale dei Lincei*, 1879.

9. In addition to the book by Posner and Raichle cited in note 8, an introduction to the principles on which modern neuroimaging studies are based can be found in the book by Pinel cited in note 1 and in Van Horn, J.D. and Gazzaniga, M.S., Databasing fMRI studies: towards a 'discovery science' of brain function, *Nature Reviews Neuroscience*, **3**: 314–18, 2002.

10. Donders, F.C., On the speed of mental processes, *Acta Psychologica*, **30**: 412–31, 1969 (originally published in 1868). Donders' method is illustrated in the book by Posner and Raichle cited in note 8.

11. Sternberg, S., The discovery of processing stages: extensions of Donders' method. *Acta Psychologica*, **30**: 276–315, 1969.

12. Farah, M.J., A picture is worth a thousand dollars, *Journal of Neuroscience*, **21**: 623–4, 2009.

13. Vul, E., Harris, C., Winkielman. P., and Pashler, H., Puzzling high correlations in fMRI studies of emotions, personality, and social cognition. *Perspectives in Psychological Science*, **4**: 274–90, 2009.

14. Bennett, C.M, Baird, A.A., Miller, M.B., and Walford, G.L. Neural correlates of interspecies perspective taking in the post-mortem Atlantic salmon: an

argument for multiple comparisons correction. Unpublished manuscript, 2009.

15. For the life and work of Camillo Golgi, see Mazzarello, P., *Golgi: A Biography of the Founder of Modern Neuroscience* (transl. A. Badiani and H.A. Buchtel), New York: Oxford University Press, 2010; see also Mazzarello, P., *Il Nobel Dimenticato. La Vita e la Scienza di Camillo Golgi*, Turin: Bollati Boringhieri, 2006.

16. Rizzolatti, G. and Sinigaglia, C., *Mirrors in the Brain: How Our Minds Share Actions and Emotions*, Oxford: Oxford University Press, 2008. Although written in a highly accessible style, this book provides an in-depth presentation of research on mirror neurons.

17. For a masterly account of autism from a neuropsychological standpoint, see Frith, U., *Autism: Explaining the Enigma*, Oxford: Blackwell, 1989. For the

relations between autism and mirror neurons, see Oberman, L.M. and Ramachandran, V.S., The simulating social mind: the role of the mirror neuron system and simulation in the social and communication deficits of autism spectrum disorders, *Psychological Bulletin*, **133**: 310–27, 2007; Hamilton, A.F.C., Brindley, R.M., and Frith, U., Imitation and action understanding in autistic spectrum disorders. How valid is the hypothesis of a deficit in the mirror neuron system? *Neuropsychologia*, **45**: 1859–68, 2007.

18. Liberman, A.M. and Mattingly, I.G., The motor theory of speech perception revised, *Cognition*, **21**: 1–36, 1985.

II
Mind, body, and explanations of behaviour

1. For an exposition of how the soul is divided into three parts: the mind, the unconscious and the

body, see Reed, E., *From Soul to Mind. The Emergence of Psychology from Erasmus Darwin to William James,* New Haven, CT: Yale University Press, 1997.

2. For a recent review of this theme, see Dovidio, J.F., Pearson, A.R., and Orr, P., Social psychology and neuroscience: strange bedfellows or a healthy marriage?, *Group Processes & Intergroup Relations,* **11**: 247–63, 2008.

3. Weisberg, D.S., Keil, F.C., Goodstein, J., Rawson, E., and Gray, J., The seductive allure of neuroscience explanations, *Journal of Cognitive Neuroscience,* **20**: 470–7, 2008.

4. Birch, S.A.J. and Bloom, P., The curse of knowledge in reasoning about false beliefs, *Psychological Science,* **18**: 382–6, 2007.

5. See Editorial: Mind games. How not to mix politics and science, *Nature,* **450**: 457, 2007; Miller, G., Growing pains for fMRI, *Science,* **320**: 412–14, 2008.

6. For a discussion on the levels of probability and the link between areas of the brain and cognitive states, see Chapter I of this book and the paper by Miller cited in note 5.

7. For further reading on the efficacy of the explanations, their credibility, and the category of 'nice to believe', see Legrenzi, P. and Johnson-Laird, P.N., The evaluation of diagnostic explanations for inconsistencies, *Psychologia Belgica*, **45**: 19–28, 2005.

8. Glimcher, P., Camerer, C.F., Fehr, E., and Poldrack, R.A., *Neuroeconomics: Decision Making and the Brain*, London: Academic Press, 2009.

9. For a discussion of data fusion, see the special issue of *Scientific American*, September 2008, and Butler, M.J.R., Neuromarketing and the perception of knowledge, *Journal of Consumer Behaviour*, **7**: 415–19, 2008.

10. For a classic text on neuroaesthetics, see Zeki, S., *Inner Vision: An Exploration of Art and the Brain*, Oxford: Oxford University Press, 1999. For further reading on neuroethics, see Farah, M.J., Neuroethics: the practical and the philosophical, *Trends in Cognitive Sciences*, **9**: 34–40, 2005; see also the journal *Neuroethics*, a forum for interdisciplinary studies in neuroethics and related issues in the sciences of the mind, edited by N. Levy and published by Springer Netherlands. The classic text on neurotheology is Newberg, A., D'Aquili, E., and Rause, V., *Why God Won't Go Away: Brain Science and the Biology of Belief*, New York: Ballantine Books, 2001. Google gives over 57 000 hits for neuropolitics; we suggest visiting www.neuropolitics.org.

11. Oxley, D., Hibbing, J.R., Miller, J.L., *et al.*, Political attitudes vary with physiological traits. *Science*, **321**: 1667–70, 2008.

12. For confusion in everyday reasoning between correlations and causal relationships, see Baron, J., *Thinking and Deciding*, Chapter 8, Cambridge: Cambridge University Press, 2000.

13. The extent to which neuropolitics has been subjected to fashionable trends is evident in the fact that the official magazine of the rigorous US Association for Psychological Science published a collection of articles in its September 2008 edition entitled 'This is Your Brain on Politics' in which D. Westen's well-known book *The Political Brain* (Public Affairs, New York, 2007) and other more recent studies are mentioned. Although the review is dedicated to the topic from cover to cover, the contents are merely a series of psychological research studies on decisions and attitudes that were trotted out again for the presidential elections in the November 2008. This all goes to show that the future has an ancient heart; the label sells the product of course, but there is little novelty in the contents!

NOTES

Conclusions

1. In the summer of 1968, the year of the great social
   protests led by those who thought that the world
   should change, a committee of the Harvard Medical
   School was working on defining the confines of the
   passage from life to death. They settled on a definition based on the extinction of cerebral activity in
   preference to heart failure or the shutdown of other
   organs. See the article 'Defining death', *Economist*,
   389: 78–9, 4 October 2008.

2. For further reading on the concept of 'bare life', we
   recommend Agamben, G., *Homo Sacer: Sovereign Power
   and Bare Life* ((transl. D. Heller-Roazen), Stanford, CA:
   Stanford University Press, 1998 and Agamben, G., *The
   Signature of All Things: On Method* (transl. L. D'Isanto
   and K. Atell), New York: Zone Books, 2009.

3. This is a fundamental point in Thaler, R. and Sunstein,
   C., *Nudge*, New Haven, CT: Yale University Press, 2008.

Thaler and Sunstein are exponents of libertarian paternalism (which is not the oxymoron it would seem to be!) and were consultants to Barack Obama in the presidential elections of 2008.

4. The dilemma facing the Catholic Church was very clearly formulated in the debate held by the Nova Spes International Foundation and published in the January–March 2008 issue of its magazine *Paradoxa*. The Gordian knot of the lay–Catholic dichotomy is individuated in the epistemological nature of the decisions to be taken. On the one hand there are the medical decisions which focus on the condition of the body and its organs, while on the other there are the epistemological–social questions concerning the well-being of the person involved, and even touching his/her relatives. The discussion of choices regarding premature babies is especially illuminating. Although this particular text is in Italian, the theme is global and once again the article 'Defining death' in the *Economist*, cited in note 1, is useful reading.

INDEX

INDEX

INDEX